Learning About Landforms

Volcanoes

Chris Oxlade

Raintree is an imprint of Capstone Global Library Limited, a company incorporated in England and Wales having its registered office at 7 Pilgrim Street, London, EC4V 6LB – Registered company number: 6695582

www.raintreepublishers.co.uk
myorders@raintreepublishers.co.uk

Edited by Rebecca Rissman, Daniel Nunn and Catherine Veitch
Designed by Steve Mead
Picture research by Elizabeth Alexander
Production by Victoria Fitzgerald
Originated by Capstone Global Library
Printed and bound in China

ISBN 978 1 4062 7227 7 (hardback)
17 16 15 14 13
10 9 8 7 6 5 4 3 2 1

ISBN 978 1 4062 7233 8 (paperback)
18 17 16 15 14
10 9 8 7 6 5 4 3 2 1

British Library Cataloguing in Publication Data
A full catalogue record for this book is available from the British Library.

Acknowledgements
We would like to thank the following for permission to reproduce photographs: Getty Images pp. 8 (Robert Frerck/Riser), 11 (Bob Hallam/Flickr), 17 (InterNetwork Media/Digital Vision), 18 (Mint Images - Frans Lanting), 20 (Philippe Bourseiller/Photonica World), 21 (Pool AVENTURIER/LOVINY/Gamma-Rapho), 27 (YOSHIKAZU TSUNO/AFP), 28 (Donna & Steve O'Meara/National Geographic), 29 (Christopher Pillitz/Photonica World); naturepl.com pp. 13 (© Juan Carlos Munoz), 19 (© Patrick Morris), 23 (© Visuals Unlimited); Robert Harding p. 10 (Juergen Richter/LOOK); Shutterstock pp. 4 (© Sunshine Pics), 22 (© Alexander Ryabintsev), 25 (© PavelSvoboda), 26 (© Danilo Ascione); SuperStock pp. 5 (Tips Images), 9 (Kerstin Langenberger/imagebroker.net), 14 (Cusp), 15 (Robert Francis), 16 (José Fuste Raga/age footstock), 24 (Robert Harding Picture Library).

Cover photograph of Gunung Bromo Crater erupting in Bromo Tengger Semeru National Park reproduced with permission of Corbis (© Michele Falzone).

Every effort has been made to contact copyright holders of material reproduced in this book. Any omissions will be rectified in subsequent printings if notice is given to the publisher.

Contents

Some words are shown in bold, **like this.** You can
find out what they mean by looking in the glossary.

What are landforms?

The surface of Earth is made up of many different landforms. There are hills, mountains, volcanoes, valleys, islands and caves.

This volcano is erupting.

Volcanoes that have not erupted for a while are called dormant volcanoes.

Volcanoes are made when hot, liquid rock **erupts**, or bursts, out of Earth. When volcanoes erupt, they are called active volcanoes.

Where volcanoes happen

The surface of Earth is called the **crust**. The crust is made up of huge rocks called **tectonic plates**. These parts of Earth are always moving.

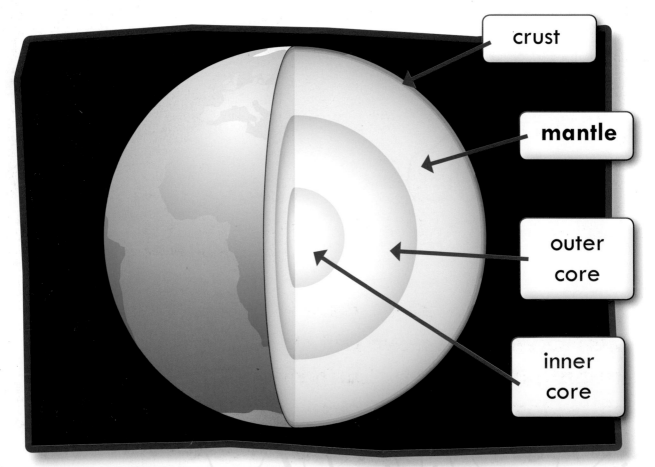

crust

mantle

outer core

inner core

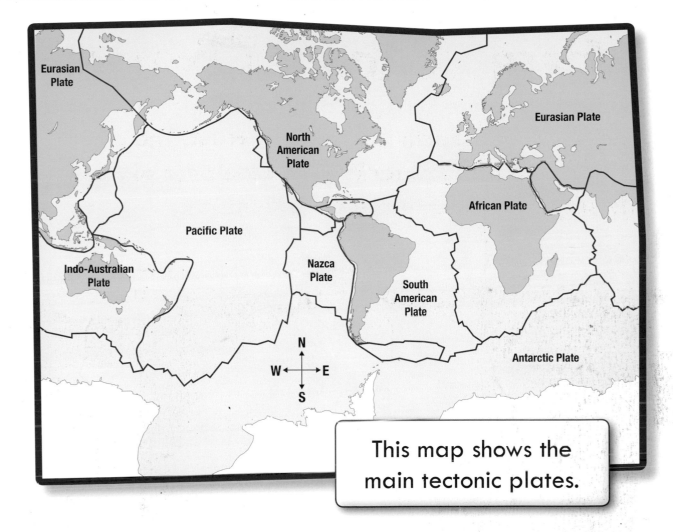

Eurasian Plate

North American Plate

Eurasian Plate

African Plate

Pacific Plate

Indo-Australian Plate

Nazca Plate

South American Plate

Antarctic Plate

N
W E
S

This map shows the main tectonic plates.

Most volcanoes are made where tectonic plates push together or move apart. Hot, liquid rock called **magma** bursts out of Earth at the edges of these plates to create volcanoes.

Where two **tectonic plates** push together, the plate underneath can melt to make **magma**. Magma is pushed up to the surface to make a volcano.

These volcanoes in Mexico were made where two tectonic plates pushed together.

This volcano in Iceland was made where two tectonic plates pulled apart.

Where two tectonic plates move apart, magma can sometimes reach the surface and create volcanoes.

Magma also bursts out of Earth at weak places in the **crust** called **hotspots.** The magma creates a volcano if it breaks out onto the surface.

This volcano on the Canary Islands is on a hotspot.

This volcanic island is in Hawaii. It is part of the United States.

Volcanoes are also made under the sea. These volcanoes are called seamounts. Volcanoes that reach the sea's surface and form islands are called volcanic islands.

Volcano parts

Magma rises from under the volcano. It flows up through a hole inside the volcano and out through **vents**. Magma is a mixture of hot, liquid **molten** rock and gas.

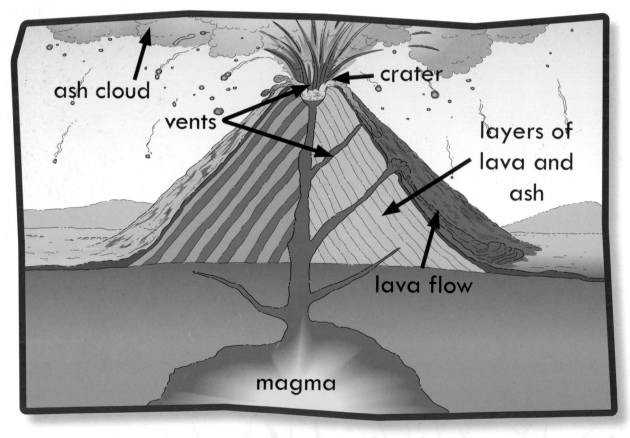

ash cloud

crater

vents

layers of lava and ash

lava flow

magma

crater

Magma sometimes comes out of a volcano in fountains of hot, runny rock called **lava.** Sometimes it comes out as ash. Lava and ash build up the walls of a **crater** at the top of the volcano.

Shield volcanoes and cinder cones

Shield volcanoes have sides that slope gently.
Shield volcanoes are made when **magma** makes
lots of runny **lava,** which flows down their slopes.

shield volcano,
Hawaii

cinder cone

Blobs of magma are sometimes thrown into the air. They cool and turn solid before they land. They are called cinders. The cinders can build up into a small volcano called a cinder cone.

Composite volcanoes

Composite volcanoes have steep sides and are cone shaped. The **lava** that comes out of composite volcanoes is thick. It does not flow like runny lava.

Mount Fuji, in Japan, is a composite volcano.

ash cloud

Composite volcanoes are made from layers of
lava and ash blasted out of the volcano. Huge
explosions blast clouds of ash many kilometres
into the air.

Volcanic flows

Volcanoes change the landscape around them, too. Hot, runny **lava** flowing down a volcano's sides is called a lava flow. It can flow for many kilometres from the volcano before it stops.

lava flow

This lava has cooled to make new rock.

new rock

As hot lava flows away from the volcano, it slowly cools. Eventually it starts to become solid. Then it stops and turns hard, forming new rock. Some lava forms smooth rocks and some forms jagged rocks.

When composite volcanoes **erupt** violently, they blast vast amounts of ash into the air. Sometimes clouds of hot ash flow down a volcano's slopes very fast, like avalanches.

Ash from the eruption of Mount Pinatubo covered the ground.

When volcanic mud stops flowing, it sets like concrete.

When volcanic ash mixes with water from rain, ice and snow, it makes volcanic mud. This mud flows from the volcano as mudflows.

Erosion and destruction

Volcanoes are worn away by **weathering** and **erosion**. Weathering is the breaking up of rocks by the weather. Erosion happens when loose rock is carried away by wind, rivers and glaciers.

gully

Weathering and erosion have made gullies in this volcano.

Mount St. Helens, Washington, USA

caldera

Composite volcanoes sometimes **erupt** with giant explosions. When this happens, the volcano is blasted to pieces. Sometimes the explosion leaves a giant hole called a **caldera**.

Volcanic features

There are usually hot rocks under Earth's surface near volcanoes. These hot rocks heat up underground water. The water comes to the surface to make boiling mud pools and hot springs.

volcanic mud pool

Geysers are spectacular fountains
of boiling water and steam.

Geysers form when water flows into holes in the
rocks and is heated by the hot rocks underground.
The water boils and some turns into steam. The
steam blasts the water back out of the hole.

Living with volcanoes

Volcanoes are dangerous landforms. **Lava** flows, falling ash and mudflows can all endanger people and their homes. In the past, thousands of people have died in **eruptions**.

Millions of people still live and work close to volcanoes.

People who live close to volcanoes often practise how to protect themselves in case of an eruption.

Many large towns and cities are very close to volcanoes. The cities grew up in these places despite the dangers.

Scientists called volcanologists study volcanoes to understand how the volcanoes **erupt** and why. Their studies are important in trying to predict when volcanoes might erupt.

Volcanologists wear special suits and use special instruments to study volcanoes.

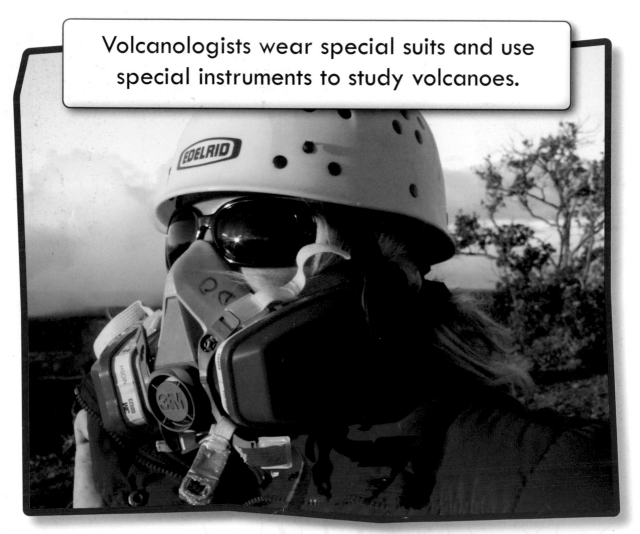

This town was destroyed when Mount Pinatubo erupted.

In 1991, volcanologists studied tiny earthquakes that showed Mount Pinatubo in the Philippines was about to erupt. They warned people, and thousands of people got to safety before Pinatubo erupted.

Glossary

caldera huge crater made when a volcano explodes violently

crater bowl-shaped hole around the opening of a volcano

crust solid, rocky skin of Earth that makes up the surface we stand on

erosion process that wears away rocks and breaks down mountains

erupt, eruption when hot ash and lava come out of a volcano

hotspots weak places in Earth's crust where magma bursts through

lava molten rock that flows from a volcano

magma molten rock under or in Earth's crust

mantle thick layer of Earth that is under the crust

molten melted

tectonic plate one of the giant pieces that form Earth's crust

vent opening that gas and liquid pass through

weathering breaking up of rocks by the weather

Find out more

Books to read

Extreme Nature: Fearsome Forces of Nature,
    Anita Ganeri (Raintree Publishers, 2012)

Eyewitness Disaster: Volcanoes! Helen Dwyer
    (Franklin Watts, 2011)

Kingfisher Readers: Volcanoes, Claire Llewellyn
    (Kingfisher, 2012)

Landform Adventurers: Volcano Explorers,
    Pam Rosenberg (Raintree Publishers, 2011)

Websites to visit
video.nationalgeographic.co.uk/video/kids/
forces-of-nature-kids/volcanoes-101-kids
Learn how volcanoes form in this interesting video.

volcano.oregonstate.edu/kids
Find out lots of facts about volcanoes on
this website.

Index